50 Premium Dishes to Eat with a Fork

By: Kelly Johnson

Table of Contents

- Filet Mignon
- Lobster Thermidor
- Duck à l'Orange
- Beef Wellington
- Rack of Lamb
- Coq au Vin
- Osso Buco
- Risotto alla Milanese
- Bouillabaisse
- Chateaubriand
- Crab Cakes
- Seared Scallops
- Lobster Ravioli
- Venison Medallions
- Truffle Mac and Cheese
- Grilled Octopus
- Beef Bourguignon

- Pan-Seared Foie Gras
- Quail with Pomegranate Glaze
- Shrimp Scampi
- Lobster Mac and Cheese
- Rack of Pork
- Miso-Glazed Black Cod
- Seafood Paella
- Braised Short Ribs
- Duck Breast with Cherry Sauce
- Braised Lamb Shanks
- Tuna Tartare
- Swordfish Steak
- Veal Saltimbocca
- Wild Mushroom Risotto
- Crab Linguine
- Seared Ahi Tuna
- Lobster Newberg
- Chicken Marsala
- Grilled Halibut

- Beef Carpaccio
- Shrimp and Grits
- Stuffed Artichokes
- Grilled Lamb Chops
- Blackened Redfish
- Scallop Ceviche
- Osso Bucco Milanese
- Lobster Bisque (with forkable garnishes)
- Pan-Roasted Duck
- Venison Stew
- Grilled Swordfish
- Roasted Bone Marrow
- Crab-Stuffed Mushrooms
- Seared Sea Bass

Filet Mignon

Ingredients:

- 2 filet mignon steaks (6-8 oz each)
- Salt and pepper
- 2 tbsp olive oil
- 2 tbsp butter
- 2 cloves garlic, smashed
- Fresh thyme sprigs

Instructions:

1. Season steaks generously with salt and pepper.
2. Heat olive oil in a skillet over high heat.
3. Sear steaks 3-4 minutes per side for medium-rare.
4. Reduce heat; add butter, garlic, and thyme.
5. Spoon melted butter over steaks while cooking 1-2 minutes more.
6. Rest steaks 5 minutes before serving.

Lobster Thermidor

Ingredients:

- 2 cooked lobster tails
- 2 tbsp butter
- 1 small shallot, minced
- 1/4 cup white wine
- 1/2 cup heavy cream
- 1 tsp Dijon mustard
- 1/4 cup grated Parmesan cheese
- Salt and pepper

Instructions:

1. Remove lobster meat from shells, chop, and set shells aside.
2. Sauté shallot in butter until soft; add wine and reduce by half.
3. Stir in cream and mustard; cook until thickened.
4. Add lobster meat, season, and heat through.
5. Fill shells with mixture, top with Parmesan.
6. Broil until golden and bubbly.

Duck à l'Orange

Ingredients:

- 2 duck breasts
- Salt and pepper
- 1/2 cup fresh orange juice
- 1/4 cup chicken stock
- 2 tbsp sugar
- 2 tbsp white vinegar
- 1 tbsp Grand Marnier or orange liqueur (optional)
- Orange zest for garnish

Instructions:

1. Score duck skin; season.
2. Cook duck skin-side down in a cold pan over medium heat until crisp, then flip and cook to desired doneness.
3. Remove duck; keep warm.
4. In same pan, caramelize sugar and vinegar.
5. Add orange juice, stock, and reduce.
6. Stir in liqueur, season.
7. Slice duck; serve with sauce and orange zest.

Beef Wellington

Ingredients:

- 1 lb beef tenderloin
- Salt and pepper
- 2 tbsp olive oil
- 1/2 cup mushroom duxelles (finely chopped mushrooms cooked down)
- 2 slices prosciutto
- 1 sheet puff pastry
- 1 egg, beaten

Instructions:

1. Season and sear beef on all sides; cool.
2. Spread mushroom duxelles over prosciutto; wrap beef tightly.
3. Roll out puff pastry; wrap beef package, seal edges.
4. Brush with egg wash.
5. Bake at 400°F (200°C) for 25-30 minutes until pastry is golden.

Rack of Lamb

Ingredients:

- 1 rack of lamb (8 ribs)
- Salt and pepper
- 2 tbsp olive oil
- 3 cloves garlic, minced
- 2 tbsp fresh rosemary, chopped

Instructions:

1. Season lamb with salt, pepper, garlic, and rosemary.
2. Heat oil in pan; sear lamb on all sides.
3. Transfer to oven at 375°F (190°C) for 15-20 minutes for medium-rare.
4. Rest before slicing.

Coq au Vin

Ingredients:

- 4 chicken thighs and legs
- Salt and pepper
- 4 slices bacon, chopped
- 1 onion, chopped
- 2 cloves garlic, minced
- 1 cup mushrooms, sliced
- 2 cups red wine
- 1 cup chicken broth
- 1 tbsp tomato paste
- 2 tsp fresh thyme

Instructions:

1. Cook bacon; remove and set aside.
2. Brown chicken in bacon fat; remove.
3. Sauté onion, garlic, and mushrooms.
4. Return chicken and bacon to pot; add wine, broth, tomato paste, thyme.
5. Simmer covered 45 minutes until tender.

Osso Buco

Ingredients:

- 4 veal shanks
- Salt and pepper
- 1/2 cup flour
- 3 tbsp olive oil
- 1 onion, chopped
- 2 carrots, chopped
- 2 celery stalks, chopped
- 1 cup white wine
- 2 cups beef broth
- 1 can diced tomatoes
- 1 tsp thyme

Instructions:

1. Season and dredge veal in flour.
2. Brown shanks in oil; remove.
3. Sauté onion, carrots, celery.
4. Deglaze with wine; add broth, tomatoes, thyme.
5. Return shanks; cover and simmer 2 hours until tender.

Risotto alla Milanese

Ingredients:

- 1 1/2 cups Arborio rice
- 4 cups chicken broth, warmed
- 1 small onion, chopped
- 2 tbsp butter
- 1/2 cup dry white wine
- Pinch of saffron threads
- 1/2 cup grated Parmesan cheese
- Salt and pepper

Instructions:

1. Soak saffron in 2 tbsp warm broth.
2. Melt butter; sauté onion until translucent.
3. Add rice; toast 2 minutes.
4. Pour wine; stir until absorbed.
5. Add broth gradually, stirring constantly, until rice is creamy and cooked.
6. Stir in saffron broth and Parmesan. Season and serve.

Bouillabaisse

Ingredients:

- 1 lb assorted fish (snapper, cod, etc.), cut into chunks
- 1/2 lb mussels, cleaned
- 1/2 lb shrimp, peeled
- 1 onion, chopped
- 2 cloves garlic, minced
- 2 tomatoes, diced
- 4 cups fish stock or seafood broth
- 1 cup white wine
- 1 fennel bulb, sliced
- 1 tsp saffron threads
- 2 tbsp olive oil
- Salt and pepper
- Fresh parsley for garnish

Instructions:

1. Heat olive oil; sauté onion, garlic, and fennel until softened.
2. Add tomatoes, saffron, and white wine; simmer 10 minutes.
3. Pour in fish stock; bring to a boil.
4. Add fish, mussels, and shrimp; cook until seafood is done (5-7 minutes).

5. Season and garnish with parsley. Serve hot with crusty bread.

Chateaubriand

Ingredients:

- 1 lb center-cut beef tenderloin
- Salt and pepper
- 2 tbsp butter
- 2 tbsp olive oil
- 2 cloves garlic, smashed
- Fresh thyme sprigs

Instructions:

1. Season beef with salt and pepper.
2. Heat oil and butter in skillet; sear beef on all sides.
3. Add garlic and thyme; baste with melted butter.
4. Finish in oven at 400°F (200°C) for 10-12 minutes for medium-rare.
5. Rest 5 minutes before slicing.

Crab Cakes

Ingredients:

- 1 lb lump crab meat
- 1/4 cup mayonnaise
- 1 egg
- 1 tbsp Dijon mustard
- 1/2 cup breadcrumbs
- 2 green onions, chopped
- 1 tsp Old Bay seasoning
- Salt and pepper
- Olive oil for frying

Instructions:

1. Mix crab meat, mayo, egg, mustard, breadcrumbs, onions, and seasoning gently.
2. Form into patties; chill 30 minutes.
3. Heat oil in pan; cook cakes 3-4 minutes per side until golden.

Seared Scallops

Ingredients:

- 12 large sea scallops
- Salt and pepper
- 2 tbsp butter
- 1 tbsp olive oil
- Lemon wedges

Instructions:

1. Pat scallops dry; season.
2. Heat oil in skillet; sear scallops 2-3 minutes per side until golden crust forms.
3. Add butter near end and baste scallops.
4. Serve with lemon wedges.

Lobster Ravioli

Ingredients:

- Fresh or store-bought ravioli stuffed with lobster
- 2 tbsp butter
- 1 clove garlic, minced
- 1/2 cup heavy cream
- 1/4 cup white wine
- 1 tbsp fresh parsley, chopped
- Salt and pepper

Instructions:

1. Cook ravioli according to package instructions.
2. In skillet, melt butter; sauté garlic.
3. Add wine and cream; simmer until slightly thickened.
4. Toss ravioli in sauce; garnish with parsley.

Venison Medallions

Ingredients:

- 4 venison medallions
- Salt and pepper
- 2 tbsp olive oil
- 2 tbsp butter
- 2 cloves garlic, smashed
- Fresh rosemary sprigs

Instructions:

1. Season medallions.
2. Heat oil in pan; sear medallions 3-4 minutes per side.
3. Add butter, garlic, rosemary; baste medallions.
4. Rest before serving.

Truffle Mac and Cheese

Ingredients:

- 8 oz elbow macaroni
- 3 tbsp butter
- 3 tbsp flour
- 2 cups milk
- 1 cup shredded sharp cheddar
- 1 cup shredded Gruyère
- 1-2 tsp truffle oil
- Salt and pepper
- 1/2 cup breadcrumbs

Instructions:

1. Cook macaroni; drain.
2. Make roux: melt butter, whisk in flour, cook 1 min.
3. Gradually whisk in milk until thickened.
4. Stir in cheeses until melted; season.
5. Toss macaroni with cheese sauce and truffle oil.
6. Place in baking dish; top with breadcrumbs.
7. Bake at 375°F (190°C) for 20 minutes until golden.

Grilled Octopus

Ingredients:

- 1 lb octopus, cleaned
- 1 lemon, sliced
- 4 cloves garlic
- 2 tbsp olive oil
- Salt and pepper
- Fresh parsley

Instructions:

1. Simmer octopus with lemon and garlic until tender (45-60 minutes).
2. Cool and cut into pieces.
3. Toss with olive oil, salt, and pepper.
4. Grill on high heat 3-4 minutes per side.
5. Garnish with parsley and serve.

Beef Bourguignon

Ingredients:

- 2 lbs beef chuck, cut into chunks
- Salt and pepper
- 4 slices bacon, chopped
- 1 onion, chopped
- 2 carrots, sliced
- 3 cloves garlic, minced
- 2 cups red wine (Burgundy preferred)
- 2 cups beef broth
- 1 tbsp tomato paste
- 1 tsp thyme
- 1 bay leaf
- 1 cup pearl onions, peeled
- 1 cup mushrooms, sliced
- 2 tbsp butter

Instructions:

1. Cook bacon; remove and set aside.
2. Brown beef in bacon fat; remove.
3. Sauté onion, carrots, and garlic.

4. Return beef and bacon; add wine, broth, tomato paste, herbs.

5. Simmer covered for 2-3 hours until beef is tender.

6. Sauté pearl onions and mushrooms in butter; add to stew before serving.

Pan-Seared Foie Gras

Ingredients:

- 4 slices foie gras (about 2 oz each)
- Salt and pepper
- 1 tbsp butter

Instructions:

1. Score foie gras lightly; season.
2. Heat skillet without oil; sear foie gras 30-45 seconds per side until golden.
3. Serve immediately with a sweet fruit compote or toasted brioche.

Quail with Pomegranate Glaze

Ingredients:

- 4 quails, cleaned
- Salt and pepper
- 1 cup pomegranate juice
- 2 tbsp honey
- 1 tbsp balsamic vinegar
- Olive oil

Instructions:

1. Season quail; sear in olive oil until golden.
2. Combine pomegranate juice, honey, and vinegar; simmer until syrupy.
3. Roast quail at 375°F (190°C) for 15-20 minutes, basting with glaze.
4. Serve drizzled with remaining glaze.

Shrimp Scampi

Ingredients:

- 1 lb large shrimp, peeled and deveined
- 4 cloves garlic, minced
- 4 tbsp butter
- 2 tbsp olive oil
- 1/2 cup white wine
- Juice of 1 lemon
- Red pepper flakes (optional)
- Fresh parsley, chopped
- Cooked pasta or crusty bread

Instructions:

1. Heat oil and 2 tbsp butter; sauté garlic until fragrant.
2. Add shrimp; cook until pink.
3. Pour in wine and lemon juice; simmer 2 minutes.
4. Stir in remaining butter and parsley.
5. Serve over pasta or with bread.

Lobster Mac and Cheese

Ingredients:

- 8 oz elbow macaroni
- 2 cups cooked lobster meat, chopped
- 3 tbsp butter
- 3 tbsp flour
- 2 cups milk
- 1 cup shredded sharp cheddar
- 1 cup shredded Gruyère
- Salt and pepper
- 1/2 cup breadcrumbs

Instructions:

1. Cook macaroni; drain.
2. Make roux: melt butter, whisk in flour, cook 1 min.
3. Gradually whisk in milk until thickened.
4. Stir in cheeses until melted; season.
5. Mix in lobster meat and macaroni.
6. Transfer to baking dish; top with breadcrumbs.
7. Bake at 375°F (190°C) for 20 minutes.

Rack of Pork

Ingredients:

- 1 rack of pork (8 ribs)
- Salt and pepper
- 2 tbsp olive oil
- 2 cloves garlic, minced
- 1 tbsp fresh rosemary, chopped

Instructions:

1. Season pork with salt, pepper, garlic, and rosemary.
2. Sear pork in olive oil until browned.
3. Roast at 400°F (200°C) for 20-25 minutes or until internal temp is 145°F (63°C).
4. Rest before slicing.

Miso-Glazed Black Cod

Ingredients:

- 4 black cod fillets
- 1/4 cup white miso paste
- 3 tbsp sake
- 3 tbsp mirin
- 2 tbsp sugar

Instructions:

1. Mix miso, sake, mirin, and sugar to make marinade.
2. Marinate cod for at least 2 hours or overnight.
3. Broil cod until caramelized and cooked through, about 10 minutes.

Seafood Paella

Ingredients:

- 1/2 lb shrimp
- 1/2 lb mussels, cleaned
- 1/2 lb clams, cleaned
- 1 cup Arborio or paella rice
- 1 onion, chopped
- 1 red bell pepper, chopped
- 2 cloves garlic, minced
- 1 tomato, diced
- 3 cups seafood broth
- 1 tsp smoked paprika
- Pinch saffron threads
- Olive oil
- Fresh parsley

Instructions:

1. Sauté onion, pepper, and garlic in olive oil.
2. Add rice, tomato, paprika, and saffron; stir.
3. Pour in broth; cook uncovered for 15 minutes.
4. Arrange seafood on top; cook until seafood is done and rice is tender.

5. Garnish with parsley.

Braised Short Ribs

Ingredients:

- 4 lbs beef short ribs
- Salt and pepper
- 2 tbsp olive oil
- 1 onion, chopped
- 2 carrots, chopped
- 2 celery stalks, chopped
- 3 cloves garlic, minced
- 2 cups red wine
- 2 cups beef broth
- 2 sprigs thyme
- 1 bay leaf

Instructions:

1. Season and brown short ribs in oil; remove.
2. Sauté onion, carrots, celery, and garlic.
3. Deglaze with wine; add broth, herbs, and ribs.
4. Cover and braise in oven at 325°F (160°C) for 2.5-3 hours until tender.

Duck Breast with Cherry Sauce

Ingredients:

- 2 duck breasts, skin on
- Salt and pepper
- 1 cup fresh or frozen cherries, pitted
- 1/4 cup red wine
- 1 tbsp balsamic vinegar
- 1 tbsp honey
- 1 tsp fresh thyme

Instructions:

1. Score duck skin; season with salt and pepper.
2. Sear duck skin-side down in a cold pan; cook until skin is crisp (6-8 min).
3. Flip and cook 3-4 more minutes for medium rare. Rest.
4. In same pan, add cherries, wine, vinegar, honey, thyme; simmer until sauce thickens.
5. Serve duck sliced with cherry sauce drizzled over.

Braised Lamb Shanks

Ingredients:

- 4 lamb shanks
- Salt and pepper
- 2 tbsp olive oil
- 1 onion, chopped
- 2 carrots, chopped
- 3 cloves garlic, minced
- 2 cups red wine
- 2 cups beef or lamb broth
- 2 sprigs rosemary
- 2 sprigs thyme

Instructions:

1. Season lamb; brown in oil, remove.
2. Sauté onion, carrots, garlic.
3. Deglaze with wine; add broth and herbs.
4. Return lamb; cover and braise at 325°F (160°C) for 2.5-3 hours until tender.

Tuna Tartare

Ingredients:

- 8 oz sushi-grade tuna, finely diced
- 1 tbsp soy sauce
- 1 tsp sesame oil
- 1 tsp lime juice
- 1/2 avocado, diced
- 1 tbsp chopped chives
- Salt and pepper
- Optional: diced cucumber, chili flakes

Instructions:

1. Combine tuna, soy sauce, sesame oil, lime juice, chives.
2. Gently fold in avocado.
3. Season; serve chilled with crackers or on a bed of greens.

Swordfish Steak

Ingredients:

- 2 swordfish steaks
- Salt and pepper
- 2 tbsp olive oil
- 1 lemon, sliced
- Fresh herbs (thyme, parsley)

Instructions:

1. Season swordfish; heat oil in skillet.
2. Cook 4-5 minutes per side until cooked through and golden.
3. Serve with lemon slices and herbs.

Veal Saltimbocca

Ingredients:

- 4 veal cutlets, pounded thin
- 4 slices prosciutto
- 8 fresh sage leaves
- 2 tbsp olive oil
- 2 tbsp butter
- Salt and pepper
- Toothpicks

Instructions:

1. Place 2 sage leaves and 1 prosciutto slice on each veal cutlet; secure with toothpicks.
2. Heat oil and butter; cook cutlets 3-4 minutes per side until browned and cooked.
3. Remove toothpicks before serving.

Wild Mushroom Risotto

Ingredients:

- 1 1/2 cups Arborio rice
- 4 cups vegetable or chicken broth, kept warm
- 2 cups mixed wild mushrooms, sliced
- 1 onion, chopped
- 2 cloves garlic, minced
- 1/2 cup dry white wine
- 3 tbsp butter
- 1/2 cup Parmesan cheese, grated
- Olive oil
- Salt and pepper

Instructions:

1. Sauté mushrooms in olive oil; set aside.
2. Cook onion and garlic in butter until soft.
3. Add rice; toast 2 minutes.
4. Pour in wine; cook until absorbed.
5. Add broth one ladle at a time, stirring, until creamy and rice is tender.
6. Stir in mushrooms and Parmesan; season.

Crab Linguine

Ingredients:

- 8 oz linguine pasta
- 1 cup cooked crab meat
- 3 cloves garlic, minced
- 1/4 cup olive oil
- 1/2 cup cherry tomatoes, halved
- 1/4 cup white wine
- 1 tbsp lemon juice
- Fresh parsley, chopped
- Salt and pepper

Instructions:

1. Cook linguine; reserve 1/2 cup pasta water.
2. Sauté garlic in olive oil; add tomatoes and cook 2 minutes.
3. Add crab, wine, lemon juice; simmer 3 minutes.
4. Toss pasta with sauce; add pasta water if needed.
5. Garnish with parsley.

Seared Ahi Tuna

Ingredients:

- 2 ahi tuna steaks
- Salt and pepper
- 2 tbsp sesame oil
- 1 tbsp soy sauce
- Sesame seeds

Instructions:

1. Season tuna; coat with sesame seeds.
2. Heat oil; sear tuna 1-2 minutes per side for rare center.
3. Drizzle with soy sauce before serving.

Lobster Newberg

Ingredients:

- 1 lb cooked lobster meat, chopped
- 3 tbsp butter
- 1/4 cup brandy or sherry
- 1 cup heavy cream
- 2 egg yolks
- Salt and cayenne pepper
- Fresh parsley for garnish

Instructions:

1. Melt butter; add brandy and flambé (optional).
2. Add cream; heat gently.
3. Whisk egg yolks; temper with cream mixture, then combine all.
4. Stir in lobster; season and warm through (do not boil).
5. Serve over buttered toast or puff pastry; garnish with parsley.

Chicken Marsala

Ingredients:

- 4 boneless, skinless chicken breasts
- Salt and pepper
- 1/2 cup flour (for dredging)
- 4 tbsp butter
- 2 tbsp olive oil
- 8 oz mushrooms, sliced
- 3/4 cup Marsala wine
- 1/2 cup chicken broth
- Fresh parsley, chopped

Instructions:

1. Pound chicken to even thickness; season and dredge in flour.
2. Heat butter and olive oil; brown chicken 3-4 min per side; remove.
3. Sauté mushrooms until browned.
4. Add Marsala wine and broth; simmer until reduced by half.
5. Return chicken to pan; cook until sauce thickens and chicken is cooked through.
6. Garnish with parsley.

Grilled Halibut

Ingredients:

- 4 halibut fillets
- Olive oil
- Salt and pepper
- Lemon wedges
- Fresh dill or parsley

Instructions:

1. Brush halibut with olive oil; season.
2. Grill over medium-high heat 4-5 minutes per side until opaque.
3. Serve with lemon and herbs.

Beef Carpaccio

Ingredients:

- 8 oz beef tenderloin, very thinly sliced
- 2 tbsp olive oil
- Juice of 1 lemon
- Salt and pepper
- Parmesan shavings
- Arugula
- Capers

Instructions:

1. Arrange beef slices on a chilled plate.
2. Drizzle olive oil and lemon juice.
3. Season; top with Parmesan, arugula, and capers. Serve immediately.

Shrimp and Grits

Ingredients:

- 1 lb shrimp, peeled and deveined
- 1 cup stone-ground grits
- 4 cups water or broth
- 4 tbsp butter
- 1 cup sharp cheddar cheese, shredded
- 2 cloves garlic, minced
- 4 slices bacon, chopped
- 2 green onions, sliced
- Salt and pepper

Instructions:

1. Cook grits according to package with water or broth; stir in butter and cheese.
2. Cook bacon until crisp; remove and set aside.
3. Sauté garlic and shrimp in bacon fat until shrimp are pink.
4. Serve shrimp over grits; garnish with bacon and green onions.

Stuffed Artichokes

Ingredients:

- 4 large artichokes
- 1 cup breadcrumbs
- 1/2 cup Parmesan cheese, grated
- 2 cloves garlic, minced
- 1/4 cup parsley, chopped
- 1/4 cup olive oil
- Salt and pepper

Instructions:

1. Trim and prepare artichokes; remove choke.
2. Mix breadcrumbs, cheese, garlic, parsley, salt, pepper, and olive oil.
3. Stuff mixture between artichoke leaves.
4. Steam or bake covered at 375°F (190°C) for 45-60 minutes until tender.

Grilled Lamb Chops

Ingredients:

- 8 lamb chops
- 2 tbsp olive oil
- 2 cloves garlic, minced
- 1 tbsp rosemary, chopped
- Salt and pepper

Instructions:

1. Marinate lamb chops with oil, garlic, rosemary, salt, and pepper for 30 minutes.
2. Grill over medium-high heat 4-5 minutes per side for medium rare.
3. Rest before serving.

Blackened Redfish

Ingredients:

- 4 redfish fillets
- 2 tbsp Cajun seasoning
- 2 tbsp melted butter

Instructions:

1. Brush fillets with melted butter; coat with Cajun seasoning.
2. Cook in a hot cast-iron skillet 3-4 minutes per side until blackened and cooked through.

Scallop Ceviche

Ingredients:

- 1/2 lb sea scallops, thinly sliced
- Juice of 3 limes
- 1/4 cup red onion, finely chopped
- 1 jalapeño, seeded and minced
- 1/4 cup cilantro, chopped
- Salt
- Avocado slices (optional)

Instructions:

1. Marinate scallops in lime juice for 15-20 minutes until opaque.
2. Mix in onion, jalapeño, cilantro, and salt.
3. Serve chilled with avocado slices.

Osso Buco Milanese

Ingredients:

- 4 veal shanks, about 1 ½ inches thick
- Salt and pepper
- Flour (for dredging)
- 2 tbsp olive oil
- 1 carrot, diced
- 1 celery stalk, diced
- 1 onion, diced
- 3 cloves garlic, minced
- 1 cup dry white wine
- 1 ½ cups beef broth
- 1 can (14 oz) diced tomatoes
- 2 sprigs thyme
- 1 bay leaf
- Zest of 1 lemon + 1 tbsp parsley (for gremolata)

Instructions:

1. Season and dredge shanks in flour. Brown in olive oil, then remove.
2. Sauté vegetables and garlic until softened.

3. Add wine; simmer and reduce. Add broth, tomatoes, herbs, and return veal.

4. Braise covered at 325°F (165°C) for 2–2.5 hours.

5. Mix gremolata (lemon zest + parsley) and sprinkle before serving.

Lobster Bisque (with Forkable Garnishes)

Ingredients:

- 1 lb lobster meat, chopped
- Lobster shells (if available)
- 4 tbsp butter
- 1 shallot, minced
- 1 carrot, diced
- 1 stalk celery, diced
- 2 tbsp tomato paste
- 1/2 cup dry sherry
- 1/4 cup flour
- 4 cups seafood or fish stock
- 1 cup heavy cream
- Salt, pepper
- Garnishes: butter-poached lobster chunks, microgreens, croutons

Instructions:

1. Sauté vegetables in butter. Add shells and tomato paste; cook 3 mins.
2. Deglaze with sherry; reduce by half. Add flour and cook 2 mins.
3. Stir in stock, simmer 30 mins. Strain and return liquid to pot.

4. Add cream and chopped lobster; season.

5. Garnish with forkable toppings.

Pan-Roasted Duck

Ingredients:

- 2 duck breasts, skin on
- Salt and pepper
- 2 sprigs thyme
- 1 tbsp butter

Instructions:

1. Score duck skin, season well.
2. Place skin-side down in a cold pan; cook until fat renders and skin crisps (6-8 mins).
3. Flip; add butter and thyme. Baste and cook 3-4 mins. Rest before slicing.

Venison Stew

Ingredients:

- 2 lbs venison stew meat, cubed
- 3 tbsp flour
- Salt and pepper
- 2 tbsp oil
- 1 onion, chopped
- 2 carrots, chopped
- 2 parsnips or potatoes, chopped
- 2 cups red wine
- 2 cups beef broth
- 2 sprigs rosemary
- 2 cloves garlic

Instructions:

1. Dredge venison in seasoned flour; brown in batches.
2. Sauté onion and garlic; deglaze with wine.
3. Add broth, herbs, meat, and vegetables.
4. Simmer covered 2–2.5 hours until tender.

Grilled Swordfish

Ingredients:

- 4 swordfish steaks
- 2 tbsp olive oil
- 1 lemon, zested and juiced
- 1 tbsp fresh oregano
- Salt and pepper

Instructions:

1. Marinate fish in oil, lemon, oregano, salt, and pepper for 30 minutes.
2. Grill 4-5 mins per side over medium-high heat.
3. Serve with lemon wedges.

Roasted Bone Marrow

Ingredients:

- 4 beef marrow bones (3–4 inches)
- Salt and pepper
- Fresh parsley, chopped
- Crusty bread, toasted
- Optional: capers, shallots, lemon zest

Instructions:

1. Preheat oven to 450°F (230°C).
2. Place bones cut-side up in a baking dish. Roast for 15-20 mins until marrow is bubbly.
3. Top with parsley and optional toppings.
4. Scoop onto toasted bread.

Crab-Stuffed Mushrooms

Ingredients:

- 20 large button mushrooms
- 1/2 lb crab meat
- 1/4 cup cream cheese
- 2 tbsp mayonnaise
- 1/4 cup Parmesan
- 1 tbsp chives
- 1/2 tsp garlic powder
- Salt and pepper

Instructions:

1. Remove stems; clean mushrooms.
2. Mix crab, cream cheese, mayo, Parmesan, chives, garlic powder.
3. Stuff mushrooms; bake at 375°F (190°C) for 20 minutes until golden.

Seared Sea Bass

Ingredients:

- 4 sea bass fillets
- Salt and pepper
- 2 tbsp olive oil
- 1 tbsp butter
- Juice of 1 lemon
- Fresh herbs (thyme, parsley)

Instructions:

1. Season fillets; heat oil in skillet.
2. Sear 3-4 mins per side until golden and cooked through.
3. Finish with butter, lemon juice, and herbs.

www.ingramcontent.com/pod-product-compliance
Lightning Source LLC
LaVergne TN
LVHW061949070526
838199LV00060B/4045